STEAM ON THE ISLE OF WIGHT

a personal journey

Bruce Oliver

NOODLE BOOKS

© Kevin Robertson (Noodle Books) and Bruce Oliver 2008

ISBN   978-1-906419-04-2

First published in 2008 by Kevin Robertson
under the **NOODLE BOOKS** imprint
PO Box 279
Corhampton
SOUTHAMPTON
SO32 3ZX

www.kevinrobertsonbooks.co.uk

Printed in England by the Alden Press

Front cover: - Ventnor, 8*th* April 1965. No 33 'Bembridge' stands under the gantry, pausing prior to rejoining its train which it has just run round.

Preceding page: - 28*th* May 1966, No 35 'Freshwater' coasts along the pier, en route to St.John's Road depot, presumably having completed a turn of duty. 35 and 36 were the final Class O2 transfers to the Island, arriving in April 1949. They were push-pull fitted to operate the Ventnor West branch. 36 'Carisbrooke', (L&SWR 198 of April 1891) had been withdrawn in June 1964 but 35 (L&SWR 181 of May 1890) lasted in service until October 1966. It was eventually cut up in May 1967. 36, meanwhile, had been dismantled in October 1965.

Rear cover: - 6*th* January 1966, Haven Street. No 24 'Calbourne' heads a freight towards Newport, photographed from a train bound for Pier Head. Little was it realized at the time that Haven Street would become 'Calbourne's' eventual home, in preservation.

(All photographs by the author.)

CONTENTS

(A list of Loco Headcodes is shown on page 39)

A Personal Journey

The transport time capsule that was steam railway operation on the Isle of Wight survived just long enough for those of us then in our early twenties, with a taste for trains, to take advantage of the independence that came with adulthood. The opportunity to pursue the quest was, nevertheless, subject to several exasperating restrictions. Principal amongst these were time and money, neither of which seemed in sufficient supply to allow many youthful targets of enthusiasm to be pursued, let alone realized.

In the 1960s, colour film was a very expensive item, as indeed were railway fares, set against 'the leisure budget' of the day. Moreover, the speed of early colour film was unimaginably slow, whereas as, forty years later, shutter speeds as fast as $1/500^{th}$ of a second are now routine, even on dull days. In the 1960s, $1/250^{th}$ of a second at quite a generous aperture was a benefit granted by high summer – and, even then, only when the sun was shining. Indeed, perhaps the greatest disadvantage of the 1960s was the sun's not infrequent reluctance to oblige photographers, in answer to their prayers. Similarly there were disappointments, only to be discovered later, arising from the photographer's own inexperience and incompetence in not setting exposures correctly. It was largely guesswork so, for every picture taken that might, at the time, have been deemed successful, there were far too many results that did not pass the test. How different things have been thirty and forty years later. Many summer days in the 1960s were grim - and cool. Thus, in 1964, with barely three years on the clock in which to gather a valedictory record of Isle of Wight steam trains in colour, it was a project that should, realistically, have been doomed from the outset.

Based in Southsea during vacations and some weekends, I had a measure of advantage inasmuch as I could opt to take a ferry with confidence - sometimes at short notice – when conditions to the south seemed to be set fair. On some occasions, however, plans were in pieces within an hour of arrival at Ryde Pier Head, clouds appearing as if from nowhere, an act of wretched cruelty inflicted upon me by that atmospheric overlord, the English Channel. Yet good days there were, not as many as I would have liked, and these brought with them opportunities not to be lost - and upon which I now reflect with eternal gratitude.

Summer Saturdays reaped the finest harvest. It was a miraculous service. To the uninformed observer, it might have appeared that resources were being stretched to breaking point. Perhaps they were but, even if this was the case, it certainly didn't show, such was the esprit de corps and efficiency of the operation. Not only was there an intense service on the Ventnor route, with some trains turned round at Shanklin, but the occasional baggage train appeared, providing back-up to brake van accommodation in the outer coaches of each passenger train set.

Passenger stock comprised non-corridor bogie carriages of both Brighton and S.E.& C.R. origin - in design and, for the most part, in construction. Easily distinguishable from each other by the geometric profile of the roof cross-section, the two designs were each engagingly attractive. Generally, the condition of stock was remarkably good, both externally and internally, given that, by 1964, time was fast running out. Also to be found were Southern Railway 4-wheeled vans, to include a bogie van of pre-grouping design, completing a scene that could, in later years, have provided a large working museum of great distinction. With such limited surviving resources, the Isle of Wight Steam Railway has itself performed a miracle in preserving the atmosphere so faithfully.

The locomotive allocation completed the pre-grouping package. By this late date, all were survivors of L.& S.W.R. Class O2, earlier representatives of Brighton design (Class E1) having disappeared during the previous decade. [Surviving members of Class A1X had returned to the mainland in 1949.] By the final months of steam operation, the number of serviceable Class O2 locomotives (memorably characterized by their enlarged coalbunkers) had been reduced by about one third, from an original stock of twenty-three locomotives. They had been delivered to the island over a period of twenty-six years, from 1923 to 1949.

Also by 1964, two lines survived in the Isle of Wight, dividing at Smallbrook Junction. These served Cowes and Ventnor from Ryde Pier Head. The line to Ventnor from Ryde enjoyed the distinc-

Left: - *Smoke-box profiles of No 21 'Sandown', nearer the camera, and No 14 'Fishbourne' at Ryde Pier Head, with arrivals from Ventnor and Cowes respectively. Note the trolley. Trolleys went to and fro across the Solent in the holds of ferries. 4th September 1965.*

tion that came with the title 'Isle of Wight Railway'. Meanwhile, remnants of the Isle of Wight Central Railway provided the connection from Smallbrook Junction to the west, viz. the Ryde and Newport and the Cowes and Newport, to give them their original titles.

The line from Ryde St John's to Shanklin opened for service on 23rd August 1864, with the extension to Wroxall and Ventnor following two years later, on 10th September 1866. The northern extension from St John's to Ryde Pier Head followed very much later, not coming into use until 12th July 1880, sixteen years after St John's had itself opened to traffic. Railway operation between Ryde and Newport commenced on 20th December 1875, while the very earliest piece in the jigsaw of Isle of Wight railway history, the line connecting Cowes and Newport, had opened over thirteen years earlier on 16th June 1862. These surviving pieces were all that remained for the railway photographer to explore, from a once more extensive system. By 1964, time was of the essence.

The line from Ryde to Cowes closed to passenger service on 21st February 1966 and, just two months later, on 18th April, services linking Shanklin with Ventnor were severed. On 18th September 1966, the section from Ryde Pier Head to Esplanade was closed, to allow work in connection with electrification to proceed unhindered. Thus, all that remained during the final three months of steam operation was the truncated section from Esplanade to Shanklin. This succumbed in the obsequies of 31st December, following which engineers took over to install the necessary infrastructure for electrification between Pier Head and Shanklin.

It is with undisguised pleasure and appreciation that one is able to record the renaissance of steam operation on the Isle of Wight. The preserved railway, now connecting Smallbrook Junction and Wootton, offers the visitor a distinctive and authentic experience in railway branch line operation. The period rolling stock is running where it belongs, while the three pre-grouping locomotives, the O2 and the two A1X Class representatives are entirely appropriate. The meticulous work undertaken, from the base at Haven Street (who would once have thought it?), to recreate a period working railway of such elegance and quality is a remarkable achievement, and one that cannot be overstated.

Bruce Oliver.

Southsea 2008.

Opposite top: - No 27 'Merstone' waits at Pier Head, platform 2, with a Cowes train. No 27, new in June 1890, entered service on the mainland as L&SWR No 184. It moved to the Island in March 1926. In 1967, it was withdrawn in January, cut up in May. 6th January 1966.

Opposite lower: - Recorded on 5th April 1966, No 31 'Chale' stands at Pier Head, platform 2, on a Ventnor service, creating atmospheric excitement. No 31 was new in April 1890, entering service as L&SWR No 180. Cut up in September 1967, it had lasted until March that year, used on electrification work. Obscured by water vapour here is tell-tale evidence of a Drummond boiler, safety valves situated in the dome.

Two views of No 16 'Ventnor', waiting in platform 2 at Pier Head on a Ventnor service, Saturday 28th May 1966. More trolleys clutter the platform, though by this time, the 1960s blue-painted B.R.U.T.E. version had reached the Island - but that nearest the camera is wooden and elderly.

Above: - No 14 'Fishbourne' projects beyond the ramp at the southern end of platform 1 at Pier Head, awaiting departure on a Ventnor train. 14 moved to the Island in May 1936, having been completed as L&SWR 178 in July 1890. It was withdrawn in January 1967 and cut up in May the same year. P.S.Ryde, built in 1937 and still with its funnel painted in traditional yellow, is here berthed alongside. 26th August 1964.

Opposite top: - On 16th August 1965, No 22 'Brading' projects beyond end of platform 2 at Pier Head on a Cowes service, perhaps also about to race the tram that is just visible. The water tank served platforms 1 & 2. 22 was new in June 1892, as L&SWR 215. At this time, No 22 was fitted with a distinctive Drummond boiler. The locomotive lasted until the very end of normal service, being withdrawn in January 1967 and cut up in May the same year.

Opposite lower: - Now preserved, No 24 'Calbourne' here heads a L.C.G.B. special on 3rd October 1965, standing in platform 4 at Pier Head. By this time, 24 had lost its brass nameplates and was finished in unlined black. New in December 1891 as L&SWR 209, the engine reached the Island in April 1925. It was officially withdrawn in March 1967, having been employed, prior to preservation, on work in connection with the change-over from steam.

Above: - The pier at Ryde has its origins in an Act of 1812. By 1865 there was in place a double-track tramway, worked over the years by both horses and steam locomotives, until electrification in 1888. From 1927 (until 1969), Drewry petrol cars and trailers operated. It was recorded here in operation on 28th May 1966.

Opposite top: - No 27 'Merstone' takes a Cowes train away from Pier Head on a January morning in 1966. The line along the Pier was brought into use on 12th July 1880, when Pier Head station was opened. Services had been opened to Esplanade three months earlier, on 8th April.

Opposite lower: - 28th May 1966. No 24 'Calbourne' leaves Pier Head on a Ventnor train. 24 is here unnamed, in its final severe livery of unlined black. The three leading vehicles are of Brighton design, betrayed by the simple circular arc as roof cross-section. Portsmouth is the distant backdrop.

Above: - On 16th August 1965, No 21 'Sandown', approaches the cross-over at Esplanade station, as it returns to St John's Road Depot. In this view, both extant paddle steamers (Ryde and Sandown) are seen, together with one of the post-war diesel boats. 21 was completed at Nine Elms in September 1891, arriving on the Island in June 1924. It was withdrawn in May 1966 but not cut up until May 1967.

Opposite top: - Another pair of views of No 16 'Ventnor', taken on the same day as the pair of views on pages 8 and 9, 28th May 1966. The engine is depicted as it makes its way along the pier towards Pier Head station. The distinction between Brighton (vehicles 2 & 3) and SE&CR (vehicles 1 & 4) roof profiles is apparent. Note that 16 has here lost its 'Ventnor' nameplates.

Opposite lower: - Looking towards Pier Head station, the pier-based signal box is seen to the left, while the stylish dome to the building forming a pier head assembly area between the platforms and the ferries completes the scene.

No 33 'Bembridge' breezes into Esplanade station, completing its journey along the pier at low tide. 8th April 1965.

On 20th February 1966, engineering work complicated operations at Esplanade in what was already a restricted area, up trains compelled to arrive on the down line. In the top view No 22's Drummond boiler is displayed to good effect, the safety valves projecting from the dome. No 22 is waiting to follow the manoeuvre of the train ahead. In the lower view the same engine, 'Brading' takes its train forward over the cross-over from Esplanade station to the pier.

Above: - On the landward side of Esplanade, No 29 'Alverstone' is about to depart on a Cowes service, 8th April 1965. 29 emerged from Nine Elms works in August 1891 as L&SWR 202. It moved to the Island in April 1926, was withdrawn in May 1966 but was not cut up until May 1967. Esplanade station opened on 05 April 1880 as a temporary terminus. Note the long macintosh, a fashion statement of the 1960s.

Opposite top: - Again operating unconventionally and which also dates the view as the same on the previous page, 20th February 1966, No 27 'Merstone' stands at the head of its train, receiving attention before proceeding northwards.

Opposite lower: - No 22 'Brading', 18 months earlier than in the previous views, arrives at Esplanade on a Ventnor train. The Southern Railway enamel station nameboard provides information in a distinctive style, unsurpassed in clarity by any subsequent design. 16th August 1965.

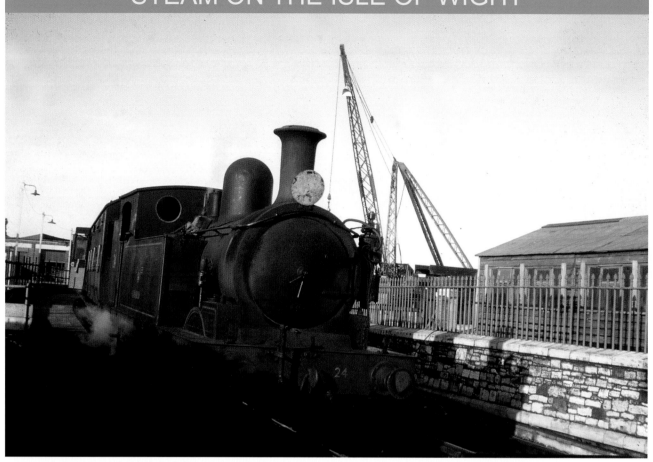

Above: *- High summer, Monday 16th August 1965, No 20 'Shanklin' climbs the 1 in 50 gradient from the tunnel to arrive in Esplanade station on a train from Ventnor.*

Opposite top: *- From summer to winter, No 24 'Calbourne' waits to leave Esplanade, wrong line, on a Ventnor train. 24 is here in lined black livery and still carries nameplates. Enlarged coal bunkers, a characteristic feature of Isle of Wight O2s, were fitted to all members of the class by the mid-1930s. The 1 in 50 descent to the tunnel (391 yards) follows almost immediately. 1st January 1964.*

Opposite lower: *- Two years later on 20th February 1966, 24 'Calbourne' again waits to leave Esplanade, here two years after the previous view. By this time, 24 had received works attention, including a full repaint in unlined black - but with its brass nameplates removed. As before, it is bound for Ventnor although from the more usual platform*

Above: - No 33 'Bembridge', near to milepost 1 and having just left the tunnel, is on its way to St.John's Road with a Ventnor train. 33 began life in August 1892, as L&SWR 218, constructed at Nine Elms like all the rest. It was withdrawn in January 1967 and cut up in May. It had moved to the Island from the mainland in May 1936, being one of the later arrivals, eight years after 32 'Bonchurch'. 27th August 1966.

Opposite top: - No 24 'Calbourne' (here with nameplates removed) descends into the tunnel at Esplanade with the L.C.G.B. special of 3rd October 1965, bound for Cowes.

Opposite lower: - On the same day as the view above of No 33 was taken, No 35 'Freshwater' rounds the corner from the tunnel, en route to St.John's Road, missing the identity of a Ventnor route white disk.

Above: - A winter timetable Cowes service arriving at St. John's Road on 8th April 1965, with No 35 'Freshwater' in charge.

Opposite lower: - No 35 'Freshwater' on a summer timetable service from Ventnor to Pier Head, about to meet No 33 'Bembridge' en route to Ventnor, approaching St. John's Road station. 4th September 1965.

Above: - Taken from the 'up' platform at St.John's Road station and looking under the road bridge, No 26 'Whitwell' enters the station on a train bound for Ventnor, 20th August 1965. 26 was delivered new in December 1891, as L&SWR 210. It was transferred to the Island in June 1925 and survived in service until May 1966. It was cut up three months later, in August 1966.

On a glorious late spring day, 28th May 1966, No 35 'Freshwater' arrives at St. John's Road, with the ex-SE&CR bogie baggage van, a vehicle converted from a carriage in 1956.

No 20 'Shanklin' takes the token at St.John's Road, prior to setting out for Cowes, 6th January 1966. Meanwhile, No 35 'Freshwater' has just arrived from the Newport direction with a short freight. Note the ex-L&SWR brake van. St John's Road opened for service on 23rd August 1864,when the line as far as Shanklin first offered the public the opportunity for rail travel. The line to Esplanade opened 16 years later.

Above: *- The outer face of the island platform at St John's Road is here seen to good effect, awning, valencing and finial providing an attractive setting in this winter view, 1ˢᵗ January 1965. The train is bound for Cowes and is headed by No 30 'Shorwell'. 30 was outshopped new in September 1892, as L&SWR 219. It arrived on the Island in April 1926, was withdrawn in September 1965 but was not cut up until November 1967.*

Opposite top: *- The station comprises three platforms, with the 'down' side an island. In this view, No 33 'Bembridge', here denied the dignified embellishment of its nameplates, arrives on a service to Shanklin. The paraphernalia of station activity proceeds, with a Pier Head bound SE&CR brake opening its doors for business. The coaching stock on the outer face of the island is parked.*

Opposite lower: *- No 27 'Merstone' runs through St.John's Road, light engine from Pier Head, returning to the depot following a turn of duty. The contents of the SE&CR brake, seen in the previous picture, have evidently been thinned in the intervening minutes. 28ᵗʰ May 1966.*

Above: - *Contrasts of darkness and light Inside St John's locomotive depot on 1st January 1965. No 22 'Brading' receives attention and is 'not to be moved'.*

Opposite top: - *St. John's Road locomotive depot was situated on the west side of the station, a two-road shed with sidings further to the west. Here No 14 'Fishbourne' and No 27 'Merstone' rest between duties; each carries a Ventnor line route disk. 1st January 1965.*

Opposite lower: - *Summer time now at the same location. No 20 'Shanklin' is found almost by itself on the shed road closest to the station. The author's mother, clad suitably in white and not one to miss an opportunity, provides occasional company for No 20. 26th August 1964.*

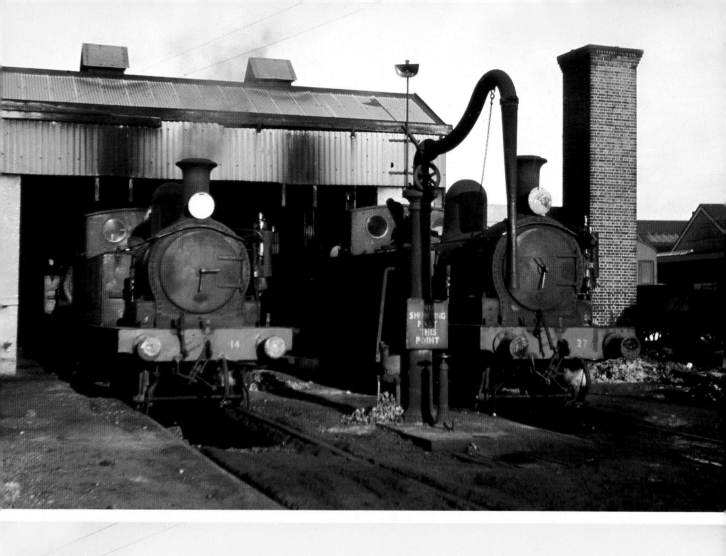

Above: - On the east side of the station at St. John's Road the works was to be found. On this occasion 20th February 1966, No 16 'Ventnor' sits beneath the hoist, its trailing set of wheels temporarily positioned at the wrong end.

Opposite: - Parked in the open air on the coaling stage line amidst a mixture of steam coal and grass, is No 35 'Freshwater'. 26th August 1964

Above: - On a bright New Years Day in 1964, No 18 'Ningwood' prepares to leave St. John's Road for Cowes, with the signal box roof as a backdrop. On the gantry, all four signals were used during the winter season, the route to Smallbrook Junction functioning as two single lines.

Opposite top: - Two years later on 6th January 1966 and another winter period freight photograph. Here No 35 'Freshwater' arrives from the Ventnor direction, with ex-L&SWR brake vans top-and-tailing just three open trucks.

Opposite lower: - During a dull spell on an August morning, No 28 'Ashey' arrives at St. John's Road with a train of locomotive coal from Medina Wharf. In contrast with the previous photograph, the gantry offers each platform only one signal, Smallbrook Junction signal box being switched into circuit. 20th August 1965.

1933 Headcodes

1   Ryde Pier Head and Ventnor (all stations) also Newport and Freshwater
2   Cowes and Ventnor via Merstone
3   Goods Trains, Light Engines and Coaching Stock only Ryde Pier Head and Ryde St John's Road.
4   Newport and Ventnor West
5   Ryde Pier Head and Cowes
6   Ryde Pier Head and Ventnor (not calling at all stations)
7   Brading and Bembridge
8   Shunting Engines

(Extract from 'The Signalling of the Isle of Wight Railways'. Published by The Signalling Record Society)

Opposite top: - *Looking back at St.John's Road station as No 14 'Fishbourne' takes away a train to Ventnor on 26th August 1964.The signal box had begun life at Waterloo Junction (East), prior to installation of colour light signalling.*

Opposite lower: - *Taken from the 'up' platform, with 'summer' gantry and signal box framing the scene, No 33 'Bembridge' waits to move on to the depot while 24 'Calbourne', 31 'Chale' and 27 'Merstone' stand defiantly in the way. 28th May 1966.*

Above: - No 22 'Brading' glides along between St. John's Road and Smallbrook Junction on a Ventnor 'fast' service. The gantry controlling the south approach to St. John's Road here is without a right-hand arm, indicating the summer timetable and double-track operation is in use. 4th September 1965.

Opposite top: - No 20 'Shanklin' makes stately progress towards Smallbrook from St. John's, 20th August 1965, with a train for Ventnor - here duty roster No.8. The smokebox betrays considerable evidence of overheating.

Opposite lower: - Taken nearer the track, not far from the site of the previous photograph, No 26 'Whitwell' charges on from Smallbrook to St. John's on the same date.

No 26 'Whitwell' rounds the bend to the south of Ryde, setting out for Cowes on a 5-coach train - three ex-SE&CR vehicles here sandwiched by two brake vehicles of Brighton design. 20th August 1965.

Recorded on 20th August 1964, No 17 'Seaview' is seen out in the country between St.John's and Smallbrook, hauling a Ventnor train. 17 was outshopped new in December 1891, as L&SWR 208. It moved to the Island in May 1930, was withdrawn in January 1967 - and was cut up the following May.

Taken at a site a few yards from that of the opposite lower view but on 26th August 1965, No 18 'Ningwood' makes a determined effort with a train bound for Ventnor. 18, as L&SWR 220, was new in September 1892. Reaching the Island in May 1930, it was withdrawn in December 1965 but was not cut up until January 1967.

Having left behind the outskirts of Ryde, No 21 'Sandown' gets to grips with a Ventnor train, carrying the disk for duty roster No.9. 4th September 1965.

Above: - No 31 'Chale' is seen here taking the Cowes line at Smallbrook Junction, 26th August 1964. The signal box at Smallbrook dates from 1926, when it was opened on 18th July.

Opposite top: - Just over a year later on 4th September 1965, No 33 'Bembridge' takes the Cowes line at Smallbrook Junction, for which route the token awaits, the locomotive crew at the ready. The headcode for Cowes line trains was a white disk above each buffer.

Opposite lower: - On the same date, No 29 'Alverstone' arrives at Smallbrook Junction from Cowes. The single line token from Haven Street is about to be surrendered.

Above: - At Smallbrook Junction, No 31 'Chale' takes the right-hand fork with a train bound for Cowes. It will have just taken the tablet for the journey to Haven Street, with Ashey the next station. 31's Drummond boiler is here betrayed by safety valves piercing the dome. 4th September 1965.

Opposite top: - Ashey opened with the line on 20th December 1875. Here No 17 'Seaview' calls en route to Pier Head, 20th August 1965. The Brighton design brake next to the engine is here an ad hoc addition, the following SE&CR vehicle being the outer brake for the carriage set.

Opposite lower: - On the same date, No 31 'Chale' stands by the platform at Ashey, en route to Cowes. The 'down' platform lost its loop status in 1926, later offering the only platform face. Prior to WWI, there had been a quarry siding from the 'down' side, leading to Ashey Down.

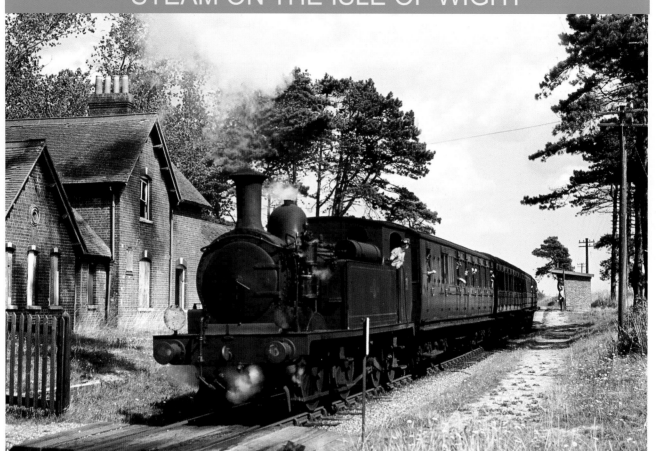

Above: - No 26 'Whitwell' hurries into Haven Street, with a train from Cowes to Pier Head in high summer, 20th August 1965. Subsequently, the centre of preservation activity, Haven Street was an island platform and a passing loop on the Smallbrook Junction to Newport route. It opened, with the line, in 1875.

Opposite top: - Ashey on 20th August 1965. No 31 'Chale' leads its train away, past the former, rather grand, station building, here in a semi-derelict condition. The track was relocated to serve the 'down' platform in 1961, leaving the 'up' platform and station building abandoned.

Opposite lower: - A few yards further west, No 17 'Seaview' drifts away from Ashey, with Haven Street in its sights, en route to Cowes again on the same date.

Above: - 6th January 1966, No 29 'Alverstone' trundles across the Medina drawbridge, on entry to Newport station. The vacant space to the right of the train had been the track bed of the line to Sandown, which closed on 6th February 1956.

Opposite top: - Looking directly towards the Medina drawbridge, the vacant former track bed to the right clearly defined, recently outshopped No 24 'Calbourne' waits to leave on a Pier Head train, 3rd October 1965..

Opposite lower: - The south end of the station on 1st January 1965. No 26 'Whitwell' waiting beneath the gantry on a train bound for Pier Head. The couple on the right are about to use the barrow crossing, in preference to the footbridge.

Above: - Looking in the north westerly direction at Newport 6th January 1966. No 20 'Shanklin' stands beneath the gantry, here reduced to a single home signal. To the right is the site of the former locomotive depot, here still in use as a yard, later the graveyard for locomotives and stock. Until March 1958 Newport South signal box had stood where the photograph was taken. With the closure of the line through to Sandown and consequent simplifying of the track and signal layout it was abolished and control at this end of the station undertaken from the remaining North cabin.

Opposite: - A somewhat intrusive view of No 26 'Whitwell' at Newport, perhaps lacking the respect accorded in the previous photograph. Newport station opened on 16th June 1862, with the commencement of services on the line to Cowes, the 'Cowes and Newport'.3rd October 1965

Above: - Mill Hill towards Newport, taken from an SE&CR design carriage window, with 22 'Brading' in charge of a train from Cowes to Pier Head. 20th February 1966.

Opposite top: - Intending passengers seemingly more interested in the photographer than the arrival of their train at Newport, 3rd October 1965. No 26 'Whitwell' entering the station from Cowes. The Southern Railway enamel station running-in board is here shewn to good effect. The fashions are well worth a second look.

Opposite lower: - A last view of No 26 'Whitwell' at Newport, here bound for Cowes but again taking water on 1st January 1965. More gantries are here in evidence, no longer fulfilling their intended purpose completely, the Freshwater branch having closed on 21st September 1953.

Above: *Following arrival at Cowes on 6th January 1966, No 20 'Shanklin' has utilised the engine release crossover at the terminal end of the platform and now runs past its stock and the small, neat signal box, soon to return to re-engage with the train. However, the carriages will have been allowed to return to the buffer stop under gravity as an independent movement.*

Opposite: *- Mill Hill, looking through the tunnel to Cowes, only about half a mile away. Opened in 1862, with the line itself, the station comprised a single platform on the west side of the track. No 20 'Shanklin' is the motive power on this occasion, 6th January 1966.*

Above: - No 24 'Calbourne' meets the end of the road at Cowes, as it prepares to run round its train. The station was, on this occasion, the focus of attention of those not there purely for the public service, a number of visitors from a Southern Counties Touring Society special also present. 20th February 1966.

Opposite top: - On the same date as the view seen above, No 22 'Brading' has here just arrived at Cowes, yet to be uncoupled prior to running round its train. The Brighton design brake next to the locomotive features panelling without moulding, an austere variant to that seen on other Brighton examples.

Opposite lower: - A few weeks earlier on 6th January 1966, No 20 'Shanklin', having arrived at Cowes, is about to detach for the run round. Alongside are a SE&CR design bogie baggage van and a standard Southern Railway 4-wheeled van. The bogie vehicle, mentioned earlier, had been converted from a carriage.

The procedure at Cowes was interesting. The locomotive, here No '20' Shanklin, first propelled its stock towards the tunnel, before returning to the buffer stop, in order to access the cross-over, seen here in the foreground. 6th January 1966.

Above: *- On 4th September 1965, No 29 'Alverstone' re-starts from the gantry controlling Smallbrook Junction, with a 'fast' service for Ventnor. Headcodes on the Ventnor line used the two central positions, above the smokebox and on the buffer beam. The standard code for Ventnor was a single disk above the smokebox. Saturday 'fast' services were indicated by an additional disk on the buffer beam but the correct code was not always carried. Some trains omitted a Brading stop, others that at Sandown. 'Short' services turned back at either Sandown or Shanklin. 15 different codes were available, using all possible combinations and permutations of the four brackets, the two either side of the smokebox having been removed. It is unlikely the one using all four, the royal code, saw any demand.*

Opposite top: *- No 33 'Bembridge' passes Smallbrook Junction with a train from Ventnor, the absence of a brass nameplate leaving an unpleasant scar. 28th May 1966.*

Opposite lower: *- On the same date as the view of No 29 on this page, No 20 'Shanklin' arrives at Smallbrook Junction with a Ventnor train. 20 was outshopped new, as L&SWR 211, in March 1892. It was one of the first pair of O2 Class locomotives to be taken to the Island, arriving there in May 1923. As was the case with so many others, it was withdrawn in January 1967 and cut up in May the same year.*

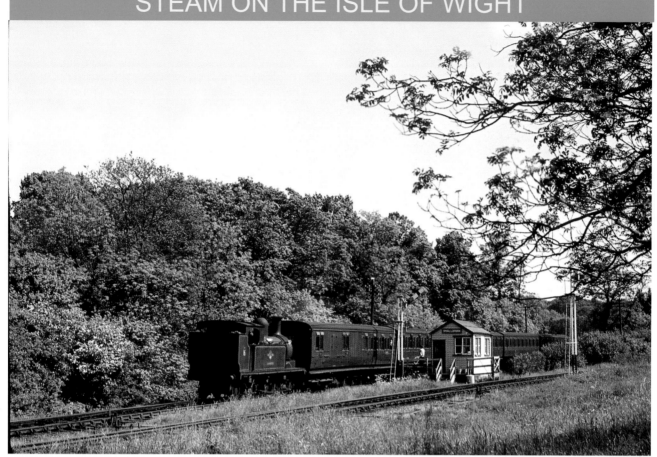

Above: - No 26 'Whitwell' creates a determined impression as it charges towards Smallbrook signal box, en route to Ventnor. 4th September 1965.

Opposite top: - No 16 'Ventnor' has just handed the token to the signalman at Smallbrook Junction and will be gaining speed for the trip to Ryde. 28th May 1966.

Opposite lower: - Trains passing at Smallbrook Junction on 4th September 1965. No 17 'Seaview' moving towards Ryde, having just left the single track section from Brading. At the inner home signals, No 35 'Freshwater' waits to gain access to the line vacated by No 17.

Above: - Three views taken on 4th September 1965. In the first No 21 'Sandown', tablet on board, proceeds towards Brading from Smallbrook signal box, on a train for Ventnor.

Opposite top: - The tablet for the single line section to Brading is seen here being taken by No 30 'Shorwell' at Smallbrook signal box. The train is a 'fast' service for Ventnor, omitting either a Brading or a Sandown stop but not both.

Opposite lower: - No 29 'Alverstone' travels between Smallbrook Junction and Brading on a Ventnor train, in a lush country setting.

Above: - Not far from Brading, No 20 'Shanklin coasts along, en route to Ventnor, 4ᵗʰ September 1965.

Opposite top: - In seemingly grimy condition and leaking steam from the cylinders,, No 33 ''Bembridge' makes its way through a bushy section on the same day.

Opposite lower: - Later in the day No 33 is recorded returning north on a 'fast' service. The paintwork bearing a smeared reference to its origins.

Above: - *Viewed from the 'up' platform at Brading on 4th September 1965. No 29 'Alverstone' waits while 30 'Shorwell' passes through on a 'fast' Ventnor service. The somewhat battered fireirons across the top of the tank top on No 29 will be noted.*

Opposite top: - *On the southern side of the bridge seen earlier, No 26 'Whitwell' approaches Brading, with Ventnor train, 27th June 1964.*

Opposite lower: *- On 4th September 1965, No 31 'Chale' runs into Brading on a Ventnor train, the little used sidings well concealed by summer growth.*

Above: - Three views at Brading on Monday 16th August 1965. No 30 'Shorwell' arrives at the station with a Ventnor train.

Opposite top: - Here we see No 21 'Sandown' arriving at the station from the south, with a train from Ventnor to Pier Head. The Southern Railway running-in board is here a prominent feature.

Opposite lower: - Approaching Brading up home signal, having come from Ventnor, is No 14 'Fishbourne'; wagons occupy the siding in the background.

PASSENGERS FOR
MUST CROSS LINE
BY THE BRIDGE

MIND THE GAP

Brading, 27th June 1964. No 35 'Freshwater' drifts into the station, the tablet for the single line section from Smallbrook Junction at the point of surrender. Earthworks for the Bembridge branch here can be discerned, the line having a right-hand fork. The branch closed on 21st September 1953.

Above: - Departing from Brading, No 30 'Shorwell' sets out for Sandown, en route to Ventnor, the former island platform clearly evident. 16th August 1965.

Opposite page: - rains meet at Sandown, 1st January 1964. No 28 'Ashey', southbound for Ventnor, is here photographed from a northbound train. 28 was built in July 1890, as L&SWR 186. It transferred to the Island in March 1926, was withdrawn in January 1967 and cut up in May that year.

Left: - Withdrawn No 32 'Bonchurch', photographed from a passing train, is found dumped at the end of a siding at Brading on 4th August 1965. 32 was new in November 1892, as L&SWR 226. It reached the Island in May 1928, was withdrawn in October 1964 and cut up in October 1965.

Above: - *Storm clouds over Sandown as No 33 'Bembridge' coasts into the station with a 4-coach train from Ventnor, a barley-twist, swan neck lamp standing sentinel over events at the south end of the station. 5th April 1966.*

Opposite top: - *A view across rusty pointwork at Sandown on 26th August 1964, with No 30 'Shorwell' drifting in on a Ventnor train. The line to Newport left the station in a north westerly direction, behind the train seen here, and had closed on 6th February 1956.*

Opposite lower: - *Another view of the northern approach to Sandown, with wagons parked adjacent to the former Newport branch, 27th August 1966.. Here No 24 'Calbourne' arrives on a Ventnor service - at a station that opened for business on 23rd August 1864.*

Above: - *On the south side of Sandown, No 22 'Brading' makes firm start on the rise to Shanklin. The gantry betrays former access to the outer face of the island platform at Sandown, once frequented by Newport services. 27th August 1966.*

Opposite top - *On the same date, No 31 'Chale' sets out for Shanklin, after a station stop at Sandown, past property that contrasts strikingly with the age of the train. It was a long climb from Sandown, through Shanklin and Wroxall, to the summit at the St.Boniface Down tunnel mouth.*

Opposite lower: - *To the left of a cluster of pine trees seen on the next page, No 35 'Freshwater' makes its way from Sandown to Shanklin again on the same day in August 1966.*

Preceding page: - *Peeping through the trunks of pine trees, No 20 'Shanklin' is seen getting to grips with the journey from Sandown to Shanklin. 27ᵗʰ August 1966.*

Above: - *On a sultry summer's day, No 35 'Freshwater' brings its train, without headcode, through Lake towards Shanklin, where passers-by stop to watch. 27ᵗʰ August 1966.*

Opposite top - *Once more on the same day and coasting past public gardens between Lake and Shanklin, No 27 'Merstone' displays the single disk for Ventnor.*

Opposite lower: - *Arriving at Shanklin and with evidence of firing just taking place, 18 'Ningwood' is bound for Ventnor, the sidings to the right evidently in commercial use. 26ᵗʰ August 1965.*

Above: - *Shanklin station opened for passenger use on 23ʳᵈ August 1864. Almost exactly a century later on 27ᵗʰ June 1964, No 27 'Merstone' and its train stand adjacent to the dark wooden canopies, unadorned by artistic valencing. The station building on the east side of the line is here glimpsed to the right.*

Opposite top: - *Against a glorious summer sky, No 17 'Seaview' has arrived at Shanklin on a terminating train. It has run round and will soon be coupling up for the return to Ryde. 27ᵗʰ June 1964. The engine would appear to have a recent works visit the smokebox having been repainted.*

Opposite lower: - *Loosing steam from the cylinders 14 'Fishbourne' departs from Shanklin and is about to tackle the rise to St. Boniface Down tunnel, visiting Wroxall en route. 20ᵗʰ August 1965.*

Above: - On a crisp January morning in 1966, No 29 'Alverstone' arrives at Shanklin on a train from Ventnor to Pier Head, while 28 Ashey waits to proceed southwards over the single line section to Wroxall. Clearly Ryde were still refurbishing coaches at this time as witness then second vehicle of the train. The line was extended from Shanklin to Ventnor in 1866, opening on 10th September that year.

Opposite: - No 22 'Brading', carrying its distinctive Drummond boiler, arrives at Shanklin on a Ventnor service, seen from the open window of an 'up' train. 8th April 1965.

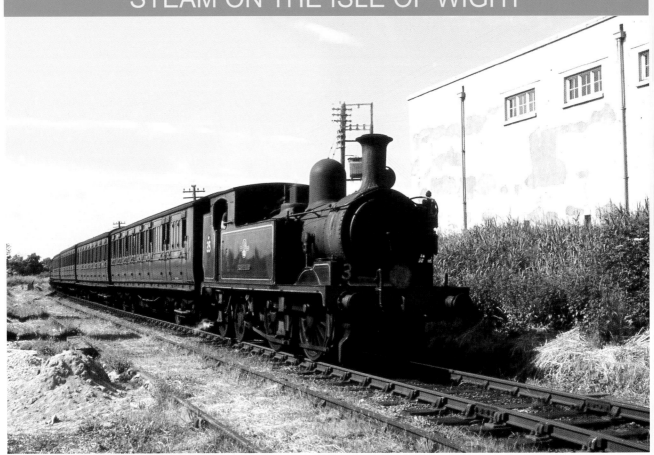

Below: - *20th August 1965, looking towards St.Boniface Down and the tunnel that took the line through to Ventnor. Here, at Wroxall, No 28 'Ashey' glides down the 1 in 88 descent from the tunnel with a train for Pier Head.*

Opposite top: - *No 35 'Freshwater' climbs the final few yards into Wroxall from Shanklin, 27th June 1964. Wroxall opened with the coming of the line in 1866. The locomotive carries the 'fast' train disk code.*

Opposite lower: - *Again No 35 'Freshwater' at Wroxall, but on 16th August 1965 again, fourteen months after its appearance in the previous photograph. It is seen leaving for Ventnor, while an 'up' train, which has recently arrived, waits in the platform.*

Page 94 top: - *The signal box at Ventnor was situated at the very mouth of the south end of the tunnel. Locomotive exhaust could linger here for many minutes, wind direction immaterial. No 33 'Bembridge' is seen in a reversing manoeuvre, soon to return to join its train. 8th April 1965.*

Page 94 lower: - *On the same date, the station area is viewed from the north, with carriages parked in a siding and an ex-L&SWR brake van standing at the outer face of the island platform. The portable bridge, seen here on the island platform, was used to connect the platforms.*

Page 95: *In the last full year of operation, No 31 'Chale', exudes steam which mingles with the smell of hot oil as it waits to leave for Ryde. 5th April 1966.*

Above: - *The low angle of sun casts shadows on 6th January 1966, as No 28 'Ashey' is recorded running around its train. Taken from the platform, not far from the station building the Southern Railway concrete running-in board usefully proclaiming 'Ventnor'. The tunnel mouth may here be clear of exhaust materials, if not the tunnel itself.*

Opposite: - *Just afterwards the same engine stands over the pit at the north end of the station. The line here has a double-sided platform, other such examples being found at Lewes (later removed), Guildford, Ascot, Norwood Junction and of course Horstead Keynes.*

Above: - *On a memorably atmospheric occasion and to prove it was not always sunny on the Island, No 31 'Chale' stands at the end of the line in teeming rain, taking water from the supply on tap. The Southern Railway enamel board above the station entrance at Ventnor explains most things, except the need to travel to Ryde for the journey to Newport, the direct line from Sandown having closed during the previous decade. 5th April 1966.*

Preceding page: - *The ex-L&SWR brake van is here seen from the southen end of the station, while No 20 'Shanklin' deals with matters of freight. 8th April 1966.*

Opposite page: - *6th January 1966, almost at the very end of the line at Ventnor, 28 'Ashey' has its smokebox cleared of ash and clinker, while its tanks are about to be replenished. Wagons complete the period scene.*

Having been prepared for the return journey, No 28 'Ashey' moves towards the buffers at Ventnor, before reversing to run round its train, for the journey back to Pier Head. It is here over 275 feet above - yet very close to - the English Channel. 6th January 1966.

On the occasion of a rail tour 3rd October 1965, Nos 14 'Fishbourne' and 24 'Calbourne' stand at Ventnor, about to double-head the return special to Ryde. Meanwhile, No 28 'Ashey' attends to the normal service train, here standing at the outer face of the island platform. The backdrop is, appropriately, the English Channel, with autumn colours completing the scene - and only 15 months of steam operation to come.